ROMANY GYPSY HOROSCOPES

JAMES PETULENGRO

SCORPIO

MILLENNIUM HOROSCOPES

2000

BROCKHAMPTON PRESS

With thanks to:
Darren Hanson, Karen Hanson, Alvin Hanson, Simon and Laurner,
Paul and Elspeth, Mark Anguluccy, Ian Sanderson, Eve, Kay, Shane,
Eric and Honer Boswell

With special thanks to my mum Leonora Petulengro and
my special friend Paula Paradema.

First published in the United Kingdom in 1999
by Brockhampton Press Limited
20 Bloomsbury Street
London WC1B 3QA
a member of the Hodder Headline PLC Group

© 1998 Brockhampton Press Limited

Designed and produced for Brockhampton Press by
Open Door Limited,
80 High Street, Colsterworth,
Lincolnshire NG33 5JA

Editing: Penny Sucharov
Design and illustration: Open Door Limited
Colour separation: GA Graphics, Stamford, UK

Printed at Oriental Press, Dubai, U.A.E.

Title: SCORPIO
ISBN: 1-86019-946-1

SCORPIO
2000

♏

CONTENTS

ROMANY PROFILE
OF SCORPIO
4

FAMOUS
SCORPIOS
8

COMPATIBILITY
WITH SCORPIO
9

DAY-BY-DAY
HOROSCOPES 2000
13

ROMANY PROFILE OF SCORPIO

Symbol:	*The scorpion*
Ruling planet:	*Mars*
Best traits:	*Self-control, patience and willpower*
Worst traits:	*Stubbornness, aggressiveness and ruthlessness*
Colours:	*Red and black*
Birthstone:	*Topaz and carnelian*
Metal:	*Iron*
Element:	*Water*
Season:	*Autumn*
Lucky numbers:	*5 and 8*
Best day:	*Tuesday*
Worst day:	*Friday*

♏

Scorpio is the eighth sign of the zodiac and governs the bladder and genitals. It is symbolised by the creature the scorpion and is one of the three water signs. Scorpio is also symbolised by the season of autumn and its influence lasts from 24th October to 22nd November.

Scorpio is ruled by the planet Mars, the planet of war, and Pluto the planet of the afterlife. People born under this sign are generally very strong-minded and opinionated and have a love of conflict. Once they have taken on an opinion, it will take a great deal of persuasion to make them change it. They also like to be in charge and tend to be very business-minded.

Scorpio people are often seen as stubborn and bossy by others. They are go-getters who are rarely satisfied with being second best. Their very strongly voiced views, which they like everyone to know, can also cause them to be quite argumentative with others who share opposing views. They will usually fight to the bitter end for the things that they believe in.

A Scorpio is a good friend to have fighting in your corner as they will protect those they care for strongly. They are also very honest people, although sometimes brutally honest. Beware of telling them too much as their honesty also means they can have trouble keeping secrets.

Although strong and aggressive on the outside, emotionally Scorpios can be quite soft, although they will rarely let it show. They have a great hatred of deceit of any kind as they will very rarely deceive others. If deceived, they will take it very badly and retaliate without remorse.

In love Scorpios are very passionate people who enjoy a good physical relationship as well as a good emotional relationship. They can, however, fall down on the romance side as their straightforward nature usually doesn't lend itself well to romantic games of the heart. They tend to be very fussy about their relationships and need a partner to stimulate them mentally as well as physically. They also have a jealous streak which can cause real problems if their chosen partner likes to flirt. However, once the Scorpio finally chooses their partner, they will very rarely change their mind.

The Scorpio parent can be very demanding of its offspring which can cause problems as the child gets older. They are, however, very protective and hold their family in high regard. They will always be there to help, although they do encourage their children to stand up for themselves from an early age.

Healthwise, the sign of Scorpio is blessed with an almost limitless source of energy which tends to ward off the majority of simple ailments. However, as the sign is linked to the bladder and reproductive organs, they should be especially careful of problems in these areas.

The Scorpio home is usually decorated very much for comfort and refuge rather than a place filled with the latest trends. Scorpios know what they like and this is definitely reflected in their home decor. They are usually not concerned about impressing others and will go to great lengths to make their homes comfortable and pleasing to themselves and their tastes.

In their spare time Scorpios tend to prefer solo hobbies and are great fans of do it yourself. They tend to like outdoor pursuits such as fishing, nature, watching and gardening. Outdoor sports such as running are also popular and their great single-mindedness means they usually excel at their chosen pastime almost to professional levels.

In the workplace the Scorpio likes to be top dog and can find it difficult being told what to do. They are hard workers who are very ambitious and like to progress. They love a job that challenges them and are rarely found in mundane or dead-end jobs which would inhibit their natural drive. They make good teachers, writers, psychiatrists, researchers, editors and are also suited to police work.

♏

FAMOUS SCORPIOS

Bram Stoker, Richard Burton, Prince Charles, John Cleese, Bill Wyman, Frank Bruno, Marie Curie, Lester Piggott, Theodore Roosevelt, Leo Trotsky, Kim Wilde, Jonathan Ross and Viscount Linley.

♏

COMPATIBILITY WITH SCORPIO

Scorpio and Scorpio

These two may know a little too much about each other to actually hit it off. However, if they do get together, this advanced insight may actually work in their favour. They will each understand the reasoning behind each other's actions which could stop some arguments from happening at all.

Score 5/10. Good if it gets of the ground.

Scorpio and Aries

This pairing can be very explosive indeed. Although a very passionate match, both of these signs like to be the one in charge and neither is inclined to back down. This relationship will always be about getting the upper hand. This definitely does not bode well for a lasting relationship.

Score 2/10. Hard-going, not an advisable match.

Scorpio and Taurus

This is a relationship which may be born more of lust than love, but which can work surprisingly well. Both of these sensual signs will have no problem giving and receiving all the physical affection that they crave. The strong will of the Taurean will also have no problem dealing with the sometimes venomous scorpion's moods.

Score 9/10. A good match in all respects.

Scorpio and Gemini

This match is not the greatest. The Scorpio tends to look for a deep relationship of sharing emotions and secrets, whereas this is the last thing on a Gemini's mind. This pair will have to work hard just to be friends, never mind lovers.

Score 2/10. Not a good pairing by any means.

Scorpio and Cancer

If they can ever actually get past each others' rigorous defences, these two will find that they have a lot in common. Both are ruled by their emotions, but in very different ways. They can, in fac,t learn a great deal from the way each other operates and can eventually make a good team.

Score 7/10. A fairly good match with a little work.

Scorpio and Leo

War is the word which generally sums up this pairing. Both of these signs like to be leader and both are very unwilling to be second. Sparks will fly as each tries to make the other submit to their own views and ways. This relationship only works on rare occasions.

Score 2/10. Not an advisable match.

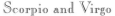

Scorpio and Virgo

These two signs are just too different to have a hope of lasting in the long term. A great deal of compromise will have to be undertaken for this match just to get off the ground. Usually, each will be going in almost exactly the opposite direction to the other, which means that they will never be on anything like the same wavelength.

Score 1/10. Not a good match.

Scorpio and Libra

This pairing is potentially problematic as the demanding Scorpio will have a tendency to walk all over the easy-going Libran. However, if the Libran is willing to fight back, there can be a good outcome for both parties.

Score 4/10. Work to be done.

Scorpio and Sagittarius

Although very different in character, this pair will be attracted to each other through pure curiosity. Sagittarius is attracted by the Scorpio's powerful personality, while the scorpion likes the liveliness of the archer's character. As long as they can work out their differences, these two won't go far wrong.

Score 8/10. A fairly good match with a bit of work.

Scorpio and Capricorn

This is an explosive combination, to say the least. These two very opinionated and strong characters will clash at almost every turn, each trying to dominate and influence the other generally to no avail. This usually means that the explosion will be over just as quickly as it started.

Score 2/10. Not a good pairing.

Scorpio and Aquarius

This will definitely not be a boring relationship, that is if each is willing to put up with the other. Both signs are very different and they will probably never understand each other. However, as they are both very active individuals, they will surely keep each other occupied.

Score 4/10. Not for those who want a quiet life.

Scorpio and Pisces

These two have a fairly good chance of lasting as the fussy Piscean will find the moody Scorpio a challenge. The Scorpio in turn will find the understanding they need in the emotional Piscean. Each will keep the other under just enough control to keep things interesting.

Score 8/10. An interesting match.

♏

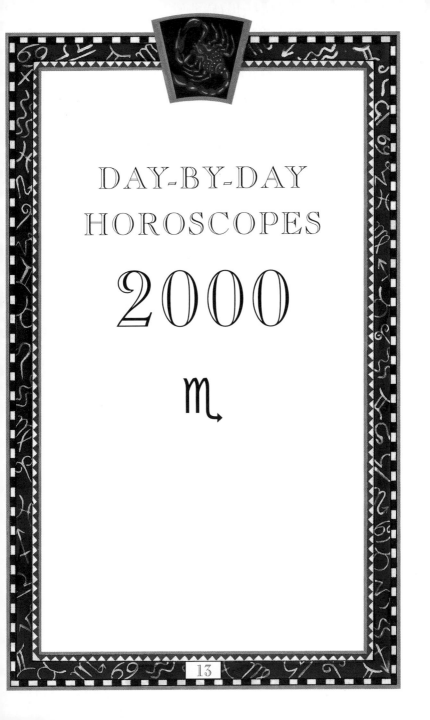

DAY-BY-DAY
HOROSCOPES

2000

♏

JANUARY

January 1st, Saturday

Happy New Year! This year will bring many good changes your way. You will be financially better off, too. Planetary influences indicate that you will be lucky in ways that you never have been before. You may need to recharge those batteries of yours as you may have been burning the candle at both ends. Take time out for a loved one as you may have neglected them a little.

January 2nd, Sunday

Try not to listen to small talk today. You may be given some very misleading information. On no account act upon this information. Today will bring good changes and planetary influences indicate that you will receive good news.

January 3rd, Monday

If you are faced with an awkward situation with a loved one, try to use another tactic. Letting your temper take control will do no good today. Try to talk things over and you'll get through to your loved one. This situation will not have a lasting effect and you'll win in more ways than one.

January 4th, Tuesday

This will be a very good day for making plans. You will hear some very good news concerning money matters and a loved one will open your eyes to a matter that has been on your mind.

January 5th, Wednesday

If you are faced with a challenge, you will enjoy what you have in front of you. Your life will take a turn for the better today and news of major changes are on the way.

January 6th, Thursday

An unexpected guest may arrive on your doorstep. If this happens, try to make them welcome as they have some very good news from which you will benefit. This will be a very lucky day for you. Be sure to jot down any numbers that come into your head as they will come in handy and bring you luck at a later date.

January 7th, Friday

A friend may come to you for your advice. Try not to take sides as their situation will soon blow over by itself. This is a good day if travelling, but plan your route with care. A loved one may also be on the warpath. The best way to handle this would be to let what they say fly over your head, as their mood will soon change.

January 8th, Saturday.

You may receive a phone call with very good news. A business proposition may be put to you. Give this some thought before you embark on any new ventures as you may already have taken on too much. You may need to pay a little attention to your finances before they get out of hand. Any problems that you discover now will be sorted out and you will benefit from this in the near future.

January 9th, Sunday

If you need to get things done, I suggest that you do them yourself today. You cannot go wrong if you are in complete charge of the situation.

January 10th, Monday

You may be faced with a little temptation. Think before you get yourself into a sticky situation. It may sound and look very exciting, but it may be in your own interest to resist as it may be too good to be true. The harder something is to obtain, the longer you keep it.

January 11th, Tuesday

There is news of money that will come your way today. Don't spend it before you actually receive it as it may take some time to reach your bank account. Lucky numbers which will help you are 5, 8 and 20. Your age will bring you luck and play a big part in your life very soon. This is the perfect day to ask someone for a favour that you have wanted doing for some time. Improvements will come from this which will make your life a little more bearable.

January 12th, Wednesday

You may feel a little puzzled over a loved one's actions, but don't worry as this will only be a passing phase. Try to look on the brighter side of life today as you will need to put yourself in a good frame of mind to be ready for a treat tonight.

January 13th, Thursday

Take friends at face value today and don't expect too much from them as you may feel a little disappointed. Try to go it alone as you will get more done. Take care not to take your temper out on your loved ones when you return home, as you will only add fuel to the fire.

January 14th, Friday

You will be pleased that this will be a very successful day. You will make great headway with any matters that you have been putting off. Also, you will receive good news concerning money matters. Love and contentment will surround you and your mind will be at peace.

January 15th, Saturday

A letter that you receive today will give you peace of mind. If you are worrying about a family matter, try not to think about it too hard as you may be worrying over something that may never happen. News of travel will come to your attention and plans that you make now will save you time in the near future.

January 16th, Sunday

This will be a perfect day to have some fun. Plan a night out on the town with a loved one or a good friend. A good time will be had by all and this will bring new friends into your life, which will open many new doors for you. It's time you got out and about a little more than you do. This will ensure that your life will spice up.

January 17th, Monday

Spend time with friends and family as this will be a day to remember. You may receive an invitation to a small party. This should be considered with care before you accept the offer. You just may meet someone who you have not seen for some time. This may add a little spark to your life, but try not to get too close to the flame as you may get your fingers burned.

January 18th, Tuesday

Planetary influences indicate that major changes are on their way, but they also indicate deceit so care must be used with people. Don't take everything for granted. What you are told may be an exaggeration of the truth, so let it go in one ear and out of the other.

January 19th, Wednesday

You may be feeling in a happy mood and you will feel on top of the world. Don't let anyone spoil your mood or bring you down. Happy times lie directly ahead and your love life will give you a big surprise. You are definitely in for a treat. Your personal life is about to take a turn for the better, but you may need to sort your finances out as you may have neglected certain aspects of your life.

January 20th, Thursday

Your business life will take a turn for the better today. You may need to backtrack and revisit some of your past before you make further progress. Money matters that have been on your mind will improve and good news comes from a family member. This will improve your life and bring much happiness.

January 21st, Friday

News of a birth may come from a friend. This will surprise not just you, but it will be a surprise to many others. However, this news will make someone very happy. Travel will come from this and someone you know will move house. You will be planning a journey, but don't rush into it as there may need to be a short delay.

January 22nd, Saturday

You may feel as if your life is on hold today in certain aspects. You may get extra inspiration from your immediate surroundings which will give you certain ideas. If you have planned travel or a business move, now is the time to get the ball rolling as planetary influences indicate that luck will be on your side.

January 23rd, Sunday

A friend may come to you with a big problem. You can give them a helping hand as they need your support at the moment. Try not to worry as this situation will soon pass and all will be well in the near future. Your love life may need a little attention as you may have pushed a loved one into the background. However, it's not too late to put things right. Spend a little time with them and hear them out. Time spent with loved ones will always pay dividends.

January 24th, Monday

You may have a lot to catch up on at home as you have been putting off those jobs that need to be done. However, now is the time to get a little more organised. You may just come across a certain item that you have mislaid. The colour red will be extra lucky for you today. You will find out what you have wanted to know about a friend. Travel is starred, so have a chat with a friend or loved one and start to plan that holiday that you need.

January 25th, Tuesday

You may be falling behind with a business project, but you will cover some good ground today. You will be in a mood to really get things done and your hard work will not go unnoticed. People near to you may be telling you their worries and troubles. However, don't take it to heart as they are probably just having a good grumble as you are such an easy person to talk to. There is news of an imminent birth and a family member may be planning a move.

January 26th, Wednesday

You may find out today the real reason why, if someone has fallen out with you for no apparent reason in the past. Don't let the past hinder your future. New friends will be made and you will find out just who is who. Real friends will come into your life and this will be the start of an exciting phase of your life.

January 27th, Thursday

You may find yourself reminiscing over matters which took place in the past. This will ensure that you do not make the same mistake twice, but you must forget the hurt that the past has caused as this is all behind you. Better times lie directly ahead. Take a good look around you and you'll realise that things are not as bad as they seem. You may just be feeling a little negative about life. It's time to recharge those batteries and look at everything with an open mind.

January 28th, Friday

Your life will return to normality today. Planetary influences have hindered you and pulled you back a little but the way ahead is clear. You may find that your life is finally moving forward and exciting matters are about to come to a head. Your life is about to move into the fast lane. Get ready for the ride of a lifetime. You will not forget it in a hurry.

January 29th, Saturday

You may be faced with a big decision today and it seems a bit of an uncompromising situation. Keep calm and all will be well. Something that you have lost out on in the past returns to your life, but this time it will be more worthwhile. Try not to snap at a loved one as they may be feeling a little pushed out. Pay them some attention and there will be no problems.

January 30th, Sunday

You may find yourself in unfamiliar surroundings today. A walk in the country or a meal in a country pub with a loved one may be on the agenda. It will give you inspiration and make your life worthwhile if you make the effort today. Listen to a loved one as they may surprise you with what they are about to tell you. This will open many doors and pave the way for your future.

January 31st, Monday

You may receive a very good offer today. Be careful as it may be too good to be true. Try not to add to your work-load as you may have too much on your plate already. Try to slow down as you may feel tired. If you are feeling a little low, try a herbal remedy. A little relaxation will do you the world of good. Maybe it's time you gave yourself a treat.

FEBRUARY

February 1st, Tuesday

Someone who wears red will bring you good luck. A big
change is foreseen and a stranger brings money closer to
your bank account. You may advance in ways that you never
thought possible and success is at your feet. Just make sure
that they stay firmly on the ground.

February 2nd, Wednesday.

A stranger who wears blue will make themselves known to
you today and put a very good opportunity your way. Try to
delay this as it may not be the right time to get into any new
business ventures. Put it on hold for a later date and you
will reap the rewards in more ways than one.

February 3rd, Thursday

A phone call that you receive today will please you greatly.
Family problems that you have encountered will be resolved
and new foundations will be laid. You must speak your mind
with a loved one as rules laid down now will save time and
trouble at a later date. Try to put money aside for some fun
later as you will get the opportunity to better your life.

February 4th, Friday

Today will bring many changes. It's time you changed your
image. Try a new style of clothing or maybe a new hair style.
This will ensure that you keep ahead and improve you image.
It will also add extra spice to your love life. Money matters will
improve and worries that you have had will fade into the past.

February 5th, Saturday

Temptation may stand in your way today. Look before you
leap. This situation may be a lot of fun, but it may

complicate your life and add to your stress. You do not really need this at the moment and you just may get caught in the act. It will do more harm than good to a relationship. You must back away from this situation at all costs as there will be a different opportunity at a later date.

February 6th, Sunday

Work may be getting you down and you may feel as if you need to change your job. Don't be too hasty. You may not think so, but all will be well and promotion will be yours for the taking. Planetary influences indicate that you will feel more at ease with your work situation. This will bring success, so stay on the same track and you will not go far wrong.

February 7th, Monday

Take time out to have a little fun. Try going somewhere that you have never been before. A shopping spree may be the answer. You may have had your eye on that certain something for some time now and this is the right time to treat yourself. You deserve it. Money matters will improve and a better position within a work situation is foreseen.

February 8th, Tuesday

Sit back and relax today and enjoy what the day brings. Take time out to relax that overactive brain of yours as you need to give it a rest. You may have overworked yourself in the recent past. Family members will bring good news and you will discover the answer to a secret.

February 9th, Wednesday

Take today as it comes and let others do the hard work. Everything should run with ease, but if it does not don't panic as it will not be as bad as it seems. A phone call that you receive at work will put you in a good mood as what you hear will really please you.

February 10th, Thursday

If a loved one is in a bad mood, do your best to let what they say fly over your head. Someone whom you hardly know will bring good news which will give you great insight into your future. This will come in very handy at a later date.

February 11th, Friday

Someone whom you rely on may just let you down, so try not to depend on them too much. However, on the whole this will be a rewarding day. Someone from the past will get in touch soon, so try to put some time to one side for old time's sake. It will be worth your while.

February 12th, Saturday

This is a good day to try to reorganise your life and get things running smoothly at home. Make a list and stick to your guns. Try not to let anything side-track you as you need to sort things out once and for all. If this is under, taken now, it will save you time and money as well as giving you a little more free time in the future.

February 13th, Sunday

Listen to what a friend has to say as this will certainly open your eyes and cast a different light on a problem that you have had. A problem shared is a problem halved. This will help you to solve certain things that you have had on your mind.

February 14th, Monday

Something that you have wanted in the past will be within your reach. You may be a little undecided about just which direction to take, but you will know deep down which choice to make. Don't be influenced by others. Follow your heart and you will have no problems.

February 15th, Tuesday

You may have to throw yourself in at the deep end with a business matter before you make any headway. This will be a day when you really get things done and you will get a project off the ground. The ball will start to roll and you will reap big rewards. Don't hesitate. Go for it.

February 16th, Wednesday

You may have to use strong words today if you want results. A tall stranger will bring you luck and the colour red will bring you money. Changes that happen around you today will be for the best in the long run, so don't panic if certain matters change. Love matters are set to improve and someone who you see through a window may just be your destiny.

February 17th, Thursday

You may ask yourself where you go from here. However, just as you give up hope of working it out, a new direction will appear right before your eyes. You must not give in to a negative frame of mind as this will do you no good. You must be positive or a good opportunity may just pass you by.

February 18th, Friday

Planetary influences indicate that you are at a turning point in your life and things in general will start to run a little more smoothly. Love is set to improve and those who are not attached will soon be singing love songs. You have luck on your side and will attract a partner.

February 19th, Saturday

You may be faced with an awkward situation today. You must use caution and choose your words with care as the person with whom you will be dealing may just be feeling a little delicate. You will make progress and this situation will go your way. The number 6 will be lucky and someone with 6 in their date of birth will bring positive changes to your life.

February 20th, Sunday

Someone whom you hold close to your heart may need some advice and you may need to find a little time for them. You may have to return a favour and this may mean that you have to put yourself out for a little while, but you will be rewarded in the near future. You never know when you just might need the favour in return.

February 21st, Monday

You may have the urge to take up some sort of sport or put a keep-fit plan together. This will do no harm and you will benefit by this if you stick to your plans. A new idea may spring into your mind. Put it down on paper as it will lead to many good things and open many new doors for you in the near future.

February 22nd, Tuesday

This week will bring many challenges, but try not to be deterred. Summon all your determination and you will win through. You will overcome any obstacles that you encounter and this will bring you more than you could ever imagine. If you have something on your mind, share it with a friend before you take action. This may help you see a problem in a different light.

February 23rd, Wednesday

Someone may really irritate today but, whatever you do, try not to play into their hands. You may just regret it after you show your feelings, so try to hide them. It will be the best policy in the long run. Turn the other cheek and you will win the day. Plans that you have made in the past will start to take shape and a good atmosphere will now surround you.

February 24th, Thursday

You may have mail delivered that you did not really want to read. However, it's not all bad news. As the day progresses you will find that you are in a very good mood and you may find that people are very helpful toward you. Don't worry as it's only the result of planetary influences.

February 25th, Friday

You will have a strange meeting with someone whom you find very attractive. You must resist temptation at all cost as you could find yourself in a very awkward situation and you could damage an existing relationship.

February 26th, Saturday

Keep your eyes open today as this will be the perfect day to pick up that bargain that you have had your eye on. Try to go out of your way a little for a loved one as they may be feeling low. Planetary influences indicate that you may feel a little down yourself, but this feeling will not last long. You have a very enjoyable evening to look forward to.

February 27th, Sunday

You may be feeling a little irritable and short-tempered. However, as the day progresses this feeling will fade away into the past, and will not return for some time. A chance meeting with an old friend is starred and money matters will improve.

February 28th, Monday

A family member may tell you all their troubles. Listen to what they have to say, but you will find out a little more than you really want to know. However, this information will come in very handy in the near future. Travel is starred and you may find yourself in a strange place. This could be the start of a very exciting adventure.

February 29th, Tuesday

You may receive a letter that brings good news. This will bring happiness into your life and will give you extra encouragement in a project that you have given up on. You are now on the right track and progress will be made.

MARCH

March 1st, Wednesday

A work associate may be trying to irritate you, but there is more to it than meets the eye. Sit back and weigh the situation up before you take action. You will overcome any problems that you face today. News of a birth is foreseen and it will bring much happiness into someone's life.

March 2nd, Thursday

A wish that you have made in the past will finally come true today. You will have a better position in life from now on. Try to have a little more understanding with a family member as you may have been a little too strict with them. Hear them out and then take the appropriate action.

March 3rd, Friday

You may need to look at a problem very deeply before you take action. A work colleague will bring good news and open your eyes to an aspect that you never thought existed. Money problems may be on your mind, but it may be time that you cut back a little on certain items that you do not really need. A child will give you inspiration and give you extra hope for the future.

March 4th, Saturday

This will prove to be a very good day financially and you will be over the moon with a partner as there will be very good news on the way. You will be in a different frame of mind and will have a different attitude with a business project. Something that you hear on the radio will inspire you and put you in a very good mood.

March 5th, Sunday

It's high time that you let down your hair and had a little fun. A night in the pub will do the trick and you never know just whom you may meet there. It may also give your professional life a boost. A chance meeting with someone whom you have had on your mind is foreseen. Good luck is just around the corner.

March 6th, Monday

If opportunity knocks, do not let it pass you by as you just may regret it at a later date. It will also be a good time for making new business deals and what happens today will govern what happens over the next few weeks.

March 7th, Tuesday

If you plan to travel by car, allow a little extra time as there may be traffic delays today. A loved one may not be to pleased with what you have in mind, but try to see things from their point of view. A little give and take will be the key to an easy day.

March 8th, Wednesday

Don't be bullied into a situation that you do not really want to be involved in. Stand your ground and don't move an inch as this time you are well and truly in the right. You will win this one. This will put a smile on your face, but try not to rub it in as it will only cause more friction.

March 9th, Thursday

You may have waited a little too long for something and now that it is within your grasp you're not really sure that it is what you really want. However, you must not pass up this opportunity as it may just have come at the wrong time. Is it really the right time to move forward?

March 10th, Friday

You may need to pay a little attention to a family matter, but this is not necessarily a bad thing. It will bring many good things into your family life. Plans made today will definitely come about and you will be closer to a personal goal.

March 11th, Saturday

Planetary influences indicate that positive changes in your personal life are about to take place. Money comes your way from an unexpected source. This would be a good time to make an investment in something that you have been told about, but could not previously afford. The ball is in your court.

March 12th, Sunday

You may find yourself tempted to get away on your own to bring a little peace and harmony in your life. Try going for a long walk, or maybe go for a long drive to a favourite place. This will give your mind a rest and bring back those good memories.

March 13th, Monday

This will be the day that your luck changes for the better and things start finally to go your way. Certain things that you have tried to do in the past have not turned out to be so easy. This will definitely make a change. More changes at work are indicated, but this time they will be to your advantage.

March 14th, Tuesday

A partner may have been treating you a little too coldly lately. You may be wondering just what they are up to. However, when it comes down to it, they are just feeling down themselves. Forget the domestic chores and pay them a little attention. It will be to your advantage and this will rekindle the flame so that it burns more brightly than when it was first lit.

March 15th, Wednesday

A travel plan may have to be changed at the last minute, but this will turn out for the best and the time that you lose will be made up later on in the day. A work colleague may help you in more ways than one. You may find it a little odd that they are going out of their way to help you, but there may be some method in their madness. Just play along with them as you will only benefit from their helping hand.

March 16th, Thursday

You may go out of your way to provoke gossip, but make sure that you tell a loved one just what you are up to and why or you may land yourself in trouble. Take a good look around you today as you might see something that you have never taken much notice of before. You will find it hard to believe that this has been right in front of you all this time. This just goes to show you that some things go unnoticed and that you should pay a little more attention to your immediate surroundings.

March 17th, Friday

You may feel like a change of scene. It may come to your attention just how much you have neglected certain people and most of all someone whom you hold very close to your heart. However, all is not lost. You can correct this if you take action now and pay some attention to those whom you have forgotten.

March 18th, Saturday

You will be in the right place at the right time today and you will be pleased with the result. You must be positive today and not afraid to air your views. Money matters will improve greatly after today's transactions and you certainly will not regret any decisions that you make today.

March 19th, Sunday

Try not to forget your friends, as planetary influences indicate that one of your friends may need a shoulder to cry on. Try to put aside a little time for them as you never know when you might need a shoulder to cry on. Go out of your way to cheer them up and you definitely will benefit from what you achieve today.

March 20th, Monday

If you are thinking of taking up a new sport or going on a diet, this is the perfect time to put a keep fit plan into action. This will ensure that you keep your looks and it will make you feel on top of the world. This is just what you need as your business life is about to enter the fast lane.

March 21st, Tuesday

If you are unattached, this may just be the day that you meet the person of your dreams as planetary influences indicate that your love life is about to liven up. Get ready for some action. Money matters may need some attention, but you will have no cause to worry as there is a surprise windfall on its way.

March 22nd, Wednesday

You may have to pick and choose your words today when talking to a stranger as you do not want to be misinterpreted. Take the right steps to impress in the right way and you will not go far wrong. A new door is about to open and you will enter a new phase of your life.

March 23rd, Thursday

You may meet a very attractive stranger and they might just make a bee-line for you. However, there will be more to it than meets the eye. Don't give in to flattery as they really don't mean what they say. Don't be taken in and you will not regret it as you will find out at a later date just what they were really up to.

March 24th, Friday

A very good day lies ahead. You will feel relaxed and happy. A phone call that you receive will be very interesting indeed, but try not to make any comments on what you are told. Love is starred well and happiness will be yours for the taking. Make sure that you get a chance to put your feet up and relax as you have a very exciting week ahead.

March 25th, Saturday

Someone will give your confidence a boost today, but try not to let it go to your head. You have a secret admirer who will make themselves known soon. Try not to get carried away with this situation as it may land you in hot water.

March 26th, Sunday

You will be faced with a very exciting challenge today. You may feel a little out of your league, but at all costs try not to show that you are feeling nervous. You will benefit by any deals that you make today and you will meet many new friends as a result of this.

March 27th, Monday

A loved one may get out of the wrong side of the bed, so ignore what they say. Don't play into their hands as they may be looking for an argument. It will not help if you go into work in a bad mood. However, a good day will be had by all and when you return home all will be forgotten.

March 28th, Tuesday

Try not to make any important decisions on the work front today as you may just end up making the wrong choice. Love matters are set to improve tenfold and news of money will come your way.

March 29th, Wednesday

Don't let a family member annoy you as they are just out for their own ends. They can sometimes be a little selfish. Look out for yourself today as you need to concentrate on more important matters. Luck will take a turn for the better and good news comes from a very strange source.

March 30th, Thursday

Listen to your heart today and you will not go far wrong. You may have a major decision to make, but you will make the right choice. Money matters that have been on your mind will sort themselves out and a friend will bring good news to you which will open a new door.

March 31st, Friday

Try not to hurt a loved one's feelings just because you don't get your own way today. It's time that you give in a little as this will not do you any harm. You are set for many changes and will receive good news of money. Someone's good fortune will benefit you in many ways.

APRIL

April 1st, Saturday

Try not to listen to a family member as they may have got their facts wrong. Follow your own advice when you face a family matter. A loved one may try to influence you, too, but stick to your own opinion and you will overcome any problems that you encounter today.

April 2nd, Sunday

If you go shopping this morning, be sure to prepare yourself for delays as planetary influences indicate that you may get held up. However, don't worry as you will have better luck in the afternoon. Try not to be too tempted to part with your money as you may end up buying things that you do not really need.

April 3rd, Monday

A friend may encounter a little misfortune, but this will not interfere with any important matter in the future. Give them a helping hand and some good advice. Your family may need some advice, too, but try not to jump to conclusions when a family member tells you a secret.

April 4th, Tuesday

Travel is indicated today. However, if you are not travelling, you may be making plans with a loved one for a holiday of a lifetime. Set the ball rolling now and you certainly will not regret it.

April 5th, Wednesday

If you are faced with a problem at work, it would be in your own interest to delegate. If you work as a team, you will get more done. Try to be a little more patient with those who are less intelligent than you as you may be running on a short fuse. Try not to let it blow or you could spoil your chances.

April 6th, Thursday

Let down that hair of yours and have some fun. Try to be a little daring and you'll be surprised at just how much fun you have. This will be a perfect day to be around your friends. Take a loved one out for a night on the town.

April 7th, Friday

If you are a little tired, make sure that you have a good rest as you have an exciting but hectic week ahead. You may get a visit from a family member and with it will come gossip. Let it go in one ear and out of the other as probably none of it will be true; just pretend that you are taking it in. Love matters will improve today and you are in for a bit of a treat tonight.

April 8th, Saturday

You may feel that today will prove to be a very good day. There is good news that a business project that has been delayed will finally start to get off the ground and certainly will be a success. Pay attention to detail as you may have missed something important. However, it will not be too late to rectify any mistakes.

April 9th, Sunday

You may have a lot of work to get through today, but try not to overdo it. Take your time and you will get more done. A phone call that you receive today will bring good news and this will be the beginning of an exciting chapter of your life. There is news of money which is on its way, but try not to spend it before you receive it.

April 10th, Monday

Someone who has done you wrong in the past will try to get around you. However, there is a method in their madness, so try not to do them any favours as they will not be returned.

Try not to let your heart rule your head as you may be in for a bit if a confusing day. You will hear some good news which will cheer you up at the end of your working day.

April 11th, Tuesday

If a bill lands on your doormat today, try not to panic as it will not be as large as you thought. If you are thinking of making major changes, now is the perfect time to do so. A loved one will try to spoil your good mood. Try not to play into their hands. Just because they got out of the wrong side of the bed this morning, it does not mean that you have to suffer. Turn a blind eye and let them get on with it.

April 12th, Wednesday

You may have other things on your mind today and find it hard to concentrate, but you must do your best not to let your thoughts take control as a very important matter may pass you by. Try to keep alert. Time will pass slowly today and you may feel as if the day will never come to an end. This may not be one of your better days, but it will not turn out as badly as you first thought.

April 13th, Thursday

If you are about to go shopping, then you are in for a treat as there will be plenty of bargains to be had. Try not to buy items that you don't really have much use for as you will finally find that special something you have had your eye on for some time. Save the best for last and save your money. Planetary influences indicate that your love life will really get a boost today.

April 14th, Friday

A day of rest lies ahead. Use this time to recharge your batteries. Spend time with a loved one; it will be worth your while. You may find yourself making plans to change your decor. However, don't get too involved or plan to change too much as you may not find the time to complete all the work as you will be very busy on the work front.

April 15th, Saturday

A busy day lies ahead and you will certainly make good progress. A close friend will ask a favour, but you may not be able to help. However, good advice will be just as good. Love matters will be on your mind, but no action must be taken today. You will know when the time is right to discuss matters of the heart.

April 16th, Sunday

Someone whom you rely on just may drop a bombshell today. You must make other arrangements. Don't rely on others. This will turn out for the best and better progress will be made. You may feel a little unsettled in your personal life, but don't worry as better times are just around the corner.

April 17th, Monday

Listen to your heart today when you are faced with a decision. New business plans will crop up out of the blue and what happens today will govern your future. Major changes are about to take place and your life will improve.

April 18th, Tuesday

You may need to give up something that you really do not want to let go of, but you stand to lose more if you keep it. Cut your ties and give it up as you will gain more in the near future. Money may change hands and you will open a new door which will bring much happiness.

April 19th, Wednesday

What you hear on the grapevine will benefit you greatly if
you act now. Someone may try to put you off, but take no
notice as they have their own agenda. Keep your ideas to
yourself as someone may use them and benefit before you
do. Secrecy is the key if you wish to advance.

April 20th, Thursday

Listen to a loved one's ideas as this will give you inspiration
for a future business project. You may find it in your own
interest to try to get closer to a loved one as certain aspects
may just be passing you by.

April 21st, Friday

You may be surrounded with people who take pleasure in
putting people down, but take no notice as they may be
feeling a little jealous about someone's success. Love
matters may need a little attention. It's time that you cut
down on a few of those luxuries.

April 22nd, Saturday

You may find out something that you have wanted to know
quite by accident. Someone will accidentally let out the
information that you have needed for some time now. Use
this to your own advantage, but try not to talk about it as
someone may try to steal your ideas. Keep your success to
yourself for a little while.

April 23rd, Sunday

You may find yourself faced with a few problems. Don't let
this get you down as you will overcome any problems that
you encounter. A loved one will be a great help and you will
find out just who your friends really are.

April 24th, Monday

You may find that you are faced with a rather exciting challenge today. What you once thought impossible will now begin to happen. However, you will be very pleased with the results of today's events. Many new doors will open and problems that you have encountered will be solved.

April 25th, Tuesday

Something may be on your mind, but you must not deal with it at this moment as you may not make any progress with it. News of money concerning a business matter will come to your attention. A family member will bring good news your way which will be to your benefit.

April 26th, Wednesday

You may be feeling a little down today. Try not to make any major decisions as planetary influences cloud your thoughts. Sit this one out and you will not regret moves that you have made. A loved one may try to influence you to do something that you really do not want to do. Give it a try and you will enjoy this new direction that you will be travelling in.

April 27th, Thursday

Take time out for yourself today as you may have neglected certain aspects of your life. You may need to look at your life from a different angle. You may see just what is wrong and what is right. This will allow you to take the correct action. Good planetary influences will soon surround you and better times lie ahead.

April 28th, Friday

If you are thinking of having a relaxing day, be prepared for someone to arrive on your doorstep. If you don't really feel like having guests, don't answer the door or you may find that your day is taken up by someone whom you have no time for.

April 29th, Saturday

Don't beat around the bush today as there will be a very good opportunity coming your way. If you get side-tracked, you could end up missing out on a very good deal, so you really need to keep your wits about you. Keep your options open too.

April 30th, Sunday

If a loved one gives you a hard time, stand up for yourself today. Don't back down as you will be in the right. If you give, in you will regret it. Stand your ground and you will overcome any problems.

MAY

May 1st, Monday

You may have a change of heart today with a business project that you have recently undertaken. Try not to act on impulse as you may regret the decisions you make today. It would not be wise to act on your feelings as planetary influences may be making you think in a negative way. Sit this one out.

May 2nd, Tuesday

Travel is indicated today and you will get the opportunity to change the direction that you are going in. Love problems that you have encountered will soon change for the better and money matters that have been on your mind will soon disappear into the past, never to return.

May 3rd, Wednesday

Someone close may need a helping hand today. You may feel that this has come at a very inconvenient time, but everything happens for a reason. Try to be patient and good will come from this as the situation will soon take a turn for the better.

May 4th, Thursday

Let your hair down today. Have some fun and let your work slip to the back of your mind. Changes will come your way and future events will please you. A good omen is starred for today and what happens will govern just what will happen in the near future.

May 5th, Friday

You may have neglected certain aspects of your life and this will need some sort of attention. Take care before you plan on spending money on extravagant items. Use caution before parting with your hard-earned cash. Make plans to improve your home, but make sure that you make a list or you could forget something very important.

May 6th, Saturday

Plan your day well, but expect things not to go according to plan. Try not to panic as this will only be temporary. However, don't get too disappointed if you do not make any real progress today. It's not all doom and gloom as there will be good news when you return home. This will surprise you in more ways than one.

May 7th, Sunday

A work situation that you have not made any headway with so far will begin to change, which will please you and take a little of the stress out of your life. A move or a change in direction is foreseen. This will bring happiness into your life. This is also a good time to meet a new love or rekindle an old flame. You are about to embark on a new venture within your love life.

May 8th, Monday

You may feel as if there is something missing in your life, but the grass always looks greener on the other side. However, there is very good news on its way concerning money matters. This will allow you to really put plans into action and improve your life immensely.

May 9th, Tuesday

Today will prove to be successful in many ways. This will be a perfect day to tackle certain matters in your life that need dealing with. Use any opportunity to discuss matters with a loved one. Your luck is set to change for the better and better times lie directly ahead.

May 10th, Wednesday

A letter that you receive may bring you to a matter that you never thought would raise its head at this moment in time. Don't worry as this is not as bad as it seems. It will work out for the better and will prove to bring good fortune your way, so try not to panic.

May 11th, Thursday

You may feel as if you just want your own company. You may be your own worst enemy if you don't spend time on your own as people will only stop you from doing what you really want to do. Speak your mind and try not to do things just to please others. It would be in your own interest if you did your own thing today. You may need time to sort certain things out, so go it alone today. It's just what you need.

May 12th, Friday

Today will make you feel on top of the world and relax your mind after the hectic week that you have just experienced. Don't worry. There will be very good news and you will feel as if progress is really being made. Sit back, relax and enjoy the day. Just let the world drift past. Love matters take a turn for the best and an enjoyable evening lies ahead.

May 13th, Saturday

Plans that you have made recently will begin to take shape and you will receive very good news concerning a business matter that has been on your mind. Someone may try to land you with extra work, but try not to take it on as you may not really have the time to cope with it. It would be best left alone for now.

May 14th, Sunday

Someone from your past may get in contact with you, but do your best to get out of a meeting that they suggest as this may only bring complications to your life. At this moment in time you really do not want anybody trying to bring you down. Remember, if it did not work in the past, it may not work in the future, so it's best left in your past.

May 15th, Monday

You may feel like a bear with a sore head this morning, but that's just Monday morning blues. This mood will soon pass and good progress will be made today. You may be in for a bit of a surprise today and you will find yourself planning something that you would not normally do. However, you'll be in for a good time and this will work out the way that you want it to, so go right ahead and don't let anybody try to change your mind.

May 16th, Tuesday

If you are faced with an uncomfortable situation at work, today is the day to confront someone who may be giving you a hard time. However, you must use clever tactics and be as polite as possible to avoid adding to the confusion that may surround you. Give your views and get things out in the open. This will clear the air.

May 17th, Wednesday

This will be a day to remember as what happens today will please you in more ways than one. Money may have been short just recently, but you will be able to be a little more generous with your cash now. Planetary influences indicate that you will undergo certain changes that can only improve your life. A friend brings good news and a family matter will be resolved.

May 18, Thursday

You may find yourself in a situation that you will enjoy and a lot of fun will be had by you and all around you. Listen to what a friend has to say about a situation that you may need a little advice on, as what they tell you will make a lot of sense.

May 19th, Friday

You may need to sit back and relax a little more to charge your batteries. You may have the time to pamper yourself and maybe put a keep-fit plan into action. This will be a good time to catch up on those jobs that you have been putting off for some time now. However, on the whole, today will certainly be a good one, So relax and enjoy yourself.

May 20th, Saturday

You may be feeling a little restless today, but you must keep you mind free from problems that you have encountered in the past as this will only spoil your good mood. Leave the past where it belongs and enjoy the day.

May 21st, Sunday

A letter that you receive today will please you greatly and this will open a door which you will want to go through. You may find that friends will get in contact with you today and you will find that they plan a really good night out and they want to include you. Make those plans and don't forget to put the dates in your diary.

May 22nd, Monday

Today may be a little hectic, but not in the way that you imagine. However, it will turn out to be a very good day. The colour green will be very lucky to you. Put on a smile and it will work wonders at work. You will find that people are attracted to you today, so use it to your own advantage.

The spotlight will be on you. If you put on the best show that you can, you will be surprised at the result.

May 23rd, Tuesday

Someone who thinks that they can take you for granted may find out just how mistaken they are today. Stand your ground and don't do anything that you don't think fitting. Today you may find out some home truths about someone. Take this information with a pinch of salt as you do not want to make any difficulties in your personal life.

May 24th, Wednesday

You will be hearing from a family member and they will bring good news about someone whom you have not seen for a long time. You will soon be seeing this person and this will be the beginning of a very good friendship.

May 25th, Thursday

You may find yourself in unfamiliar surroundings today and a family outing is foreseen. Take care with your money as you will be very tempted to spend it. A family member may try your patience, but at all costs try not to let them annoy you as this will only make matters worse.

May 26th, Friday

A day of relaxation lies ahead. You will be pleased that you finally have a little peace and quiet in your home. Use this time to think about the coming week and your thinking will be crystal clear. You will also be in for a bit of a treat tonight, so be prepared for a good time.

May 27th, Saturday

You may be told a secret today, but try not to believe it as it is only idle talk and there will be no truth in what you are told. If you repeat it, you will only be passing on misleading information. Keep it to yourself for a while. The truth will soon come into the open and clear away all the rumours that may be flying around.

May 28th, Sunday

You may feel a little on the down side and think of giving up. However, don't worry as you will be the receiver of some rather exciting news which will soon cheer you up and change your mood. Planetary influences indicate that there will be very big changes about to take place.

May 29th, Monday

Someone may offer their advice today. This may be very misleading as it probably will be in their interest only. It would be to your advantage if you stick to your own advice today. Love problems that you have recently encountered will improve and you will have less to worry about.

May 30th, Tuesday

You may be thinking of having a good spring clean today. However, before you throw anything out, have a good look at it. You'll find that you will save yourself time and money, so make sure that you have a good look before you give anything away.

May 31st, Wednesday

Be careful not to get yourself into a situation that will not be easy to get out of. Think with care before you take action as you may regret the result. Under no circumstance let your heart rule your head as you stand to lose more than you will gain.

JUNE

June 1st, Thursday

Try to put others' feeling first, before you hurt a loved one. You may be feeling rather selfish, but try to place your own needs last. If you do as you please, it will only land you in trouble.

June 2nd, Friday

If you have been thinking about embarking on a new venture, this is not the day to start it. You need to sit back, relax and let the day slip past. Your loved one may need a little attention. Any time spent with a loved one will be time well spent.

June 3rd, Saturday

A tall stranger may enter your life today. Be careful as you will be tempted to have a little fun. By all means have fun, but try not to let it get out of hand. Money matters will improve and a new chapter of your life is about to begin.

June 4th, Sunday

You may be burning the candle at both ends. It may be time to slow down a little. You will need all the rest that you can get as your life will soon be entering the fast lane. This will bring a lot of exciting challenges in your life. Loved ones will be proud of what you are doing as you are set for success.

June 5th, Monday

You will feel like a new person today and will discover things about others and notice things that had previously passed you by. You seem to be attracting others and you may feel that this is bad timing as you have a lot on your mind at the moment and better things to spend your time on. Decline any offers with grace. Walk away from them. You are not missing out on much.

June 6th, Tuesday

Keep your eyes open today as there will be a bargain to be had. This will be the time to spend those pounds and you will certainly get value for money. Spend a little on your loved one and it will give you not only peace of mind but fewer problems in the near future.

June 7th, Wednesday

You may have a lot on your mind and it's high time you said what you think. Share your thoughts with family members and friends. This is sure to clear the air. You may need to organise your life and put certain plans that you have made into action.

June 8th, Thursday

You may find yourself running around trying to get certain jobs done and not thinking about what you really should be doing. Throw down your tools, or cleaning rags or stop washing that car. Go out and have some fun. Those jobs can wait for another day.

June 9th, Friday

This has been a very odd week and you may still be attracting people, but not those whom you want to attract. Don't worry as the person of your dreams will soon come into your life. For those who have partners this will be a time when your relationship will become more intense and you will become closer than you have been for some time.

June 10th, Saturday

Numbers will play a big part in your life today. The number twelve brings you good luck. Your luck takes a turn for the better today. Your love life is set to improve and you will soon be mixing with people with whom you certainly want to make friends.

June 11th, Sunday

If you are thinking about changing your career, leave any actions to a later date. Planetary influences indicate that bigger and better things are to come. A better offer will come your way, so hang back for a little while and you certainly will not fail.

June 12th, Monday

You may feel as if you will never get through the amount of work that you have. However, keep on going and don't give in as it will pay good dividends. A friend may need a shoulder to cry on. You may feel that they have chosen a very inconvenient time, but try to set a little time aside for them and you will not regret it. This favour will be repaid in other ways.

June 13th, Tuesday

Someone who may have done you a bad turn in the past will try to right their wrong. Don't be too hard on them as their intentions are genuine. Give them a second chance as they will not betray you again.

June 14th, Wednesday

You will certainly get though plenty of work. It will be a very productive day and good progress will be made in more ways than one. You will find that a family member is on your mind, but don't worry as you will receive very good news concerning the family member that you were worrying about.

June 15th, Thursday

Try to resist those bargains that you do not really need or want. Keep your money in your pocket today as you will have better things to spend it on soon. A letter that you receive today will inspire you and alert you to a situation. It will give you the answer to the problems that have been on your mind.

June 16th, Friday

You may be feeling a little blue today, but don't worry as it's only the result of planetary influences. If you are feeling a little irritable, try not to take it out on anybody as this will only add fuel to the fire. As the day progresses your mood will lift and you'll see the world for what it really is. Loved ones are set to please you, but try not to take them for granted.

June 17th, Saturday

If you have planned a day out, it will certainly turn out to be a very good day. Be sure to make time to make a loved one feel special as this will keep you in their good books. You can use today to lay foundations for your future. Plan with care, but be sure that you ask a loved one what their views are or you could cause an argument.

June 18th, Sunday

This will be the perfect day to advance in your career. Push yourself forward and you will not go far wrong. Take extra care with a work associate and keep your ideas to yourself as someone else may take all the credit. A good day will be yours but you must use certain clever tactics to get through the day with ease.

June 19th, Monday

Money matters may need attending to and this would be the perfect day to do it. It may also be time to think about a new bank account or maybe a savings plan. A close friend will be nearby to advise you on certain matters. Love looks promising today and you'll be the centre of attention tonight.

June 20th, Tuesday

Listen to what others have to say today as what you hear in a strange room will benefit you greatly. You may pick up on a good idea which will cause your life to take a different turn. This will definitely be for the better.

June 21st, Wednesday

This may be a good day to find out certain things that you have wanted to know but did not want to ask in case you upset things. However, this is the day to find out and you'll be more than pleased with what you discover. There is news of money that may come your way. Try not to spend it before you actually receive it.

June 22nd, Thursday

You may find yourself falling in love all over again. If you are unattached, you could bump into your soulmate, so keep your eyes open. This will be a very lucky day for you and it will prove to be very successful.

June 23rd, Friday

You may find that certain aspects of your life are changing. However, everything happens for a reason and you will not be unhappy about the changes that take place. You will hear news of someone from your past, but it would not be to your advantage to try to get in touch with them. Let sleeping dogs lie.

June 24th, Saturday

Take time out today to do those jobs that desperately need doing as you may not really get the chance to do them in the near future. Be sure to sort out that paperwork, too, as you just may have forgotten something very important.

June 25th, Sunday

Today will be full of adventure not to mention a little romance. You may also find yourself falling for a stranger. However, you may never see this person again so make sure that you exchange names and, of course, addresses. You may not see this person for a while, but they will get in contact eventually.

June 26th, Monday

You will be faced with changes on the work front today but don't let this put you off as this will work out to your advantage in the long run. Pay attention to detail as this will come in quite handy at a later date. Someone may try to put you off accepting a certain offer that you have received, but try to use your own judgement.

June 27th, Tuesday

You may feel a little let down and, after all that excitement yesterday, you find it very hard to concentrate. However, you must do your best as you should try not to let other matters slip. You should be ahead with your work and finally making progress.

June 28th, Wednesday

Someone on the work front may be talking nonsense, or that may be your opinion. However, pay attention as they may give you some very important information. Friends will play a major part in your life today, so be prepared for a phone call.

June 29th, Thursday

Today will be full of surprises. There will be lots of ups and downs, but eventually it will calm down. This afternoon you will have the chance to get your own back on someone, and you certainly will have the last laugh.

June 30th, Friday

You may have made arrangements for this evening, but you may find that certain details have changed. Don't worry as you'll still have a good time. Try a new venue or make an extra effort to please a loved one. This will pay dividends.

JULY

July 1st, Saturday

What you see on TV will interest you greatly and give you inspiration for a future project. However, you must find time to relax as you have had a hectic week. News will come from a close family member and you may have to change some of your plans.

July 2nd, Sunday

You may be thinking about taking up a hobby that you have admired for some time. However, you may find that it turns out to be a little more expensive than you first thought. Try not to let the money side of the matter put you off as you will find that it is more than worth the expense.

July 3rd, Monday

If a loved one gets out of the wrong side of the bed, you must not to get upset as this will only add fuel to the fire. It would be to your advantage to try to ignore their remarks and you'll find out what is really annoying them.

July 4th, Tuesday

A child will bring much happiness into your life today, but this child may not be yours. They will also give you the inspiration that you have been looking for. A change for the better is foreseen and you'll be in for a very real surprise.

July 5th, Wednesday

Listen to what a family member has to say as they may be trying to put a very good offer your way. Try not to be stubborn, and above all try not to make any hasty moves. Today will prove to be a good day for sorting out any long-standing problems that you have.

July 6th, Thursday

You may have a very good reason to celebrate today. Maybe it's your own celebration or one for someone close to you; whichever it is, it will be an enjoyable day. Open a bottle of the best or treat yourself. You may find that you have far more fun than you first thought.

July 7th, Friday

You may be faced with a task that you think impossible. However, give it a go and you'll be surprised just what you can do when you put your mind to it. Someone close will certainly be proud of you and this will add to the cool image that you have. A friend will bring news of someone from your past, but it may not be what you anticipated. You will be in for a surprise as someone may try to walk back into your life.

July 8th, Saturday

You may find yourself in very strange surroundings, but this will be quite pleasant. You will be able to relax without anybody irritating you. Peace and harmony will be yours for the taking and you will have the time of your life. Get ready for some great fun.

July 9th, Sunday

You may find yourself in a new situation. Try not to let a new venture scare you into backing out. This will open many new doors for you and will certainly bring more contentment into your life.

July 10th, Monday

You may be feeling a little down today as someone near to you may be having better luck than you are. However, it will soon be your turn and you will get what you want A little patience is needed and it will all work out for the best.

July 11th, Tuesday

A new door opens and you may be faced with a decision. Think carefully before you make any drastic moves as you may regret any move that you make today. Follow your instincts and stick by your decision.

July 12th, Wednesday

You may be delayed with a business project that you are involved in, but take this time to re-assess the situation. If someone asks a favour, try to decline as you need to pay a little more attention to your own personal needs.

July 13th, Thursday

Good news lands on your doorstep today and this will place you in a different frame of mind. You will feel more contented after today has passed and happiness will lie at your feet.

July 14th, Friday

You may be running around in circles, but you must slow down and relax as you'll get more done in the long run. Take care with a loved one today as they may be feeling a little run down. You can improve the situation by paying more attention to them. This will ensure that the day runs smoothly.

July 15th, Saturday

Today will be full of surprises and planetary influences indicate that your love life will improve in more ways than one. You will feel better not only with your present situation but in yourself.

July 16th, Sunday

Something that you have on your mind may be troubling you. The best thing to do is to ask a stranger's advice. At least you will get an honest opinion. Take a little care whom you tell your secrets to as the people near to you today are not very good at keeping secrets. Tell someone whom you hardly know and this way it will not come back via someone else.

July 17th, Monday

Today marks a turning point in your life. Your life is about to change in many ways and you'll be more than pleased with what is about to take place. You will improve your position in many ways and your personal life also takes a turn for the better.

July 18th, Tuesday

This would be a good time to buy a lottery ticket or have a small gamble. However, don't get too carried away as there are only small wins to be had. Animals will play a big part in your life and a recent buy will turn out better than first thought.

July 19th, Wednesday

Today holds the key to a secret and you'll certainly find out the answer to some of your questions. After today you will certainly not be still in the dark. Look toward the better things in life and try to be positive and you will overcome any problems that come your way.

July 20th, Thursday

You may be surrounded by strangers and it will be really enjoyable. You will be meeting many new people and at least one will stay in your life for quite a long time. Today will have a very good feel about it and you'll be more than pleased with what is accomplished today.

July 21st, Friday

You may need some advice today. Try to ask an older member of the family or someone whom you trust a great deal. Where there's a will there's a way. You will overcome any difficulties that you encounter.

July 22nd, Saturday

Don't feel low as certain matters may be weighing you down. Today will be more than just full of surprises. Someone will help you in more ways than one, so keep smiling as you will be contented with your position at the end of the day.

July 23rd, Sunday

Your life may seem as if it is running a little too fast for you at present. You may also feel as if there have been too many changes in your life. However, you will feel more settled in your mind. Changes are about to make you happy and you will never look back as the future holds many good things.

July 24th, Monday

A good day lies ahead and you will feel on top of the world. Money matters are looking better and you can see that your life is on the up and up. Love matters are set to improve, too, and what happens tonight will keep you cheerful for the next few months.

July 25th, Tuesday

If you wake up and remember a vivid dream, be sure to write it down on paper as what lies in your dreams will have a meaning in the near future. Strangely, the coming events will be totally unlike those of your dream.

July 26th, Wednesday

You may need to take a new direction within your working life and this will make sure that you keep on top of things. You may need to make certain changes to keep up with the times, but this will ensure that you stay up there where you want to be.

July 27th, Thursday

You may be feeling a little tired of the company around you, but new people will influence you and your life will take a turn for the better on the work front. Your personal life will improve and you will be moving in different circles.

July 28th, Friday

It may not be a good idea to play games of chance today. Keep your money in your pocket; that is the best place for it. After today is out, planetary influences indicate that your luck will improve and a loved one will bring good news concerning a family member.

July 29th, Saturday

Your life is now heading in the right direction, so try not to be too keen to make a lot of changes. Think things through before making hasty decisions and this will ensure that no mistakes are made.

July 30th, Sunday

You will receive a surprise phone call today and what you are told will please you. Tackle the problem head on and things will not seem as bad as you first thought. Be careful in whom you place your confidence as you may be putting your trust in the wrong person.

July 31st, Monday

You have been keeping a secret from a loved one. Maybe it's time to come clean and this will be the perfect time to do so. This will certainly clear the air and make room for future events. Something that you have been wanting will come into your possession today and it will make life a little more pleasant. Others will look on with envy.

AUGUST

August 1st, Tuesday

Listen carefully to what a loved one has to say and you will be very encouraged about what the future may bring. Make some plans now and follow them closely and everything will work out as you imagine.

August 2nd, Wednesday

A work colleague may have it in for you today. Try your best to keep your cool and things will not get out of hand. On the whole you will have a pleasant day and you may receive an invitation to a rather unusual event. You must attend at all costs as this will be more than just the usual gathering.

August 3rd, Thursday

It may come to your attention that someone close may need a helping hand. This will alert you to a situation you never dreamed would occur. However, all will be well in the end. Your personal life will take a turn for the better and good news awaits you.

August 4th, Friday

You may be out hunting for bargains and you'll definitely find then today. You will be surrounded with plenty of choice, but you may feel confused over just what you actually want to buy. Have a good look around before you part with any money as you never know what is around the next corner.

August 5th, Saturday

You will have a bit of an eye-opener today, but you may also find out just who your real friends are. Try not to look shocked as you may be turning your back on someone who you thought would be in your life for a long time. Everything happens for a reason and you will gain a better friend.

August 6th, Sunday

You may feel as if something is missing from your life, but try not to look in the wrong places. You may end up with more than you have bargained for. You may be a little vulnerable and you must pull back from this situation.

August 7th, Monday

A good opportunity may come your way. Before you turn it down you must look at it from all sides and weigh up the positive and the negative points. If it looks good, take this offer and consider the benefits. This will be a time when you change your direction. In one way or another it will be very productive.

August 8th, Tuesday

Planetary influences indicate that you will encounter a good turn in your life. You will be feeling better and more comfortable in your present situation. The working side of your life looks very promising and you will not regret any changes that you make now.

August 9th, Wednesday

You may find yourself in unfamiliar territory. Don't let this panic you, or at least don't let it show if it does. You will now find that things in general may be a little hectic, but the pressure will ease off and you will find that you are on the right track.

August 10th, Thursday

You may need to pay a little more attention to yourself as you may have been neglecting yourself. It may be time to give yourself a treat, maybe a new image or a new outfit of clothes. You may find that you are attracting others and you will be in the spotlight for a little while.

August 11th, Friday
You may feel as if your life is on hold today, and you may feel as if you are waiting for something to happen. However, it's just that things in general are going well and they may seem too good to be true at the moment. Try not to worry as nothing is going to go wrong. Things will run smoothly and you will not find yourself in any unexpected situation.

August 12th, Saturday
You may have to look back into your past to find the answer to a problem that you have on your mind. You will find the answer and will make good progress today. The colour blue will be lucky and will be a big influence in your life.

August 13th, Sunday
You may have cause for a small celebration today. You will enjoy family and friends' company and it looks as if a family outing is on the cards. This will be a real eye-opener, but don't let certain matters put you off. You will have not just a good day but also a very enjoyable evening.

August 14th, Monday
A very unusual day lies ahead. Certain happenings may puzzle you, but try not to let your imagination run away with you. You will see things for what they really are and you'll be amazed with what has been going on right under your nose. You will find it quite amusing.

August 15th, Tuesday

If you are driving today, make sure that you do not exceed the speed limits as you never know who may be on the look out. Be extra careful as you may end up with a fine. This can be avoided if you watch your speed when driving.

August 16th, Wednesday

You may prove someone wrong today. Stand your ground and don't let anyone change your mind as today you do know what you are talking about. Don't give in just for the sake of peace. As for the romantic side of your life, the planets are on your side, So if you have been thinking about making a move, this will be a good time to do so.

August 17th, Thursday

At this present time you will benefit from plans that you have made in the past and your personal life should now be on an upward turn. Money that changes hands will be very beneficial to you in the coming months and secure your immediate future.

August 18th, Friday

You may get the better of someone who has crossed you in the past. Try not to rub it in too much as what happens to them will not be pleasant. Your fate lies in your own hands today and you are finally in control of your life.

August 19th, Saturday

A day out will do you the world of good. Try going for a drive, or a day out in the country will be very pleasant. If you are thinking of making plans to move home, this could be the right time to look into things. Planetary influences indicate that you will have some sort of change on the home front. It may be just a change of wallpaper or a move of house. You will certainly know which one it will be.

August 20th, Sunday

You may feel a little restless and in need of a change of surroundings. This feeling will not last long as it's only caused by the influence of the planets. Love surrounds you today and someone of your dreams may just walk into your life very soon.

August 21st, Monday

If you are planning to travel, this will be the perfect time to take a trip to the travel agent. Try not to let them persuade you into a cheap deal, as if you take it, you will not be pleased with the offer. Take time to think things through and you will not regret turning down a bargain.

August 22nd, Tuesday

There will be a change with your work and this will be beneficial to you once it is up and running. A stranger will give you good advice and point you in the right direction. If you have been worried about the romantic side of your life, this will be a time when things will all fall into place and the ball will be in your court.

August 23rd, Wednesday

You may think that you are a little tied down with certain aspects of your life. However, this is far from the truth as your situation will prove to be more than good in the near future. Look at other people's lives before you start to be worried about your own.

August 24th, Thursday

You may have the weight of someone else's problems on your shoulders, but you must not take these on board or to heart. You can make a great difference to their life if you give them the right advice. This will ensure that you do not carry their stress and worries.

August 25th, Friday

Take time out for a loved one today as a partner may feel a little neglected. This will be a positive day with a positive outcome. A new chapter of your life is about to begin and it may turn out to be more than just an ordinary day.

August 26th, Saturday

You will find yourself doing the odd job that needs attention, but try not to overstretch yourself as you need some rest. Don't let a close member of your family take you for granted. If you let them get away with it now, they may take you for granted in the near future.

August 27th, Sunday

Someone's attitude may really annoy you and really try your patience. It would be in your own interest to speak your mind as they may be a little jealous of you. That is their problem, not yours. Try to turn a blind eye after you have made your point.

August 28th, Monday

You may be asked to do something very out of the ordinary today and you'll be amused at just what you get yourself in to. Today will be very relaxed and there will be a lot of fun. Let your hair down and relax with the company around you. You will not forget today in a hurry.

August 29th, Tuesday

Take a good look around you and you'll be surprised at what you take for granted. You may feel a little stuck in a situation, but you'll soon move forward into better things. Try not to be impatient as you'll soon be moving into the fast lane.

August 30th, Wednesday

Someone may be quick to criticise you today, but let this fly over your head. You must not play into their hands. Use the situation and you'll come out on top. Love matters may need some attention and you'll find that you may have been missing out on certain matters.

August 31st, Thursday

You may have a bit of a wait on your hands. If you expect people to rush around and get things done, don't bank on it. The only person whom you can rely on is yourself. However, you will get through the day with ease and will be in for a rather interesting evening. You'll be in for a very good treat.

SEPTEMBER

September 1st, Friday

You'll be amazed with just what takes place today. You will be over the moon with the news that you receive. A letter that you receive today may unsettle you, but this will be sorted out in a very short space of time. A loved one comes to your rescue and all will be well.

September 2nd, Saturday

You may have a deadline to meet. Try not to panic as you will get through and meet your target. Try not to be too hard on yourself as you will deserve a pat on the back. Pamper yourself and do something that you really enjoy doing.

September 3rd, Sunday

Play a joke on a loved one or a family member and you'll have more fun than you have had in a long time. This will start the day off in the right way. Try to look at certain matters critically. A phone call that you receive today will open your eyes and you will find out something that you have wanted to know for some time now. Use this information to your own advantage.

September 4th, Monday

A different light will be cast on a work situation and you'll be very surprised at what the result will be. To your surprise this will work out to your advantage. Don't worry over money matters as your purse will be full, but unfortunately not bottomless. Spend your money with care.

September 5th, Tuesday

Someone may try to take advantage of your good nature. Don't let them. You will see straight through them and you should use this situation to obtain information that you need before gently letting them down.

September 6th, Wednesday

You may find that you are in new surroundings and in new company. You may find that you are feeling a little shy and you are not showing yourself at your best. Summon some confidence and you'll soon be the centre of attention. Try not to show off as you may give someone the wrong impression.

September 7th, Thursday

Look back into your past and try to remember the good times. This will put you in a good mood. You will need to be at your best as you will need to be on top form today. This will leave a long-lasting impression on someone in power who could help you in the near future. Advancement is foreseen and you will be offered a better position or another type of work.

September 8th, Friday

Don't rely on electrical items today as this may be a day when the things you use the most let you down. This goes for people, too, so try to manage without either. If you need some career advice, you may need to speak to someone that has no experience in your field. You may need to have a little break and do your own thing.

September 9th, Saturday

Love matters really play a major part in your life today and will work out to suit you. You will not have to change any big decisions that you have already made. You may also feel that you are not advancing as fast you wish, but your life will soon speed up in the right areas.

September 10th, Sunday

You should really put your heart and soul into your work today as you will have the opportunity to better your position and get the right people on your side at the right time. You may reach heights that you never thought possible. Whether at home or at work, whatever you are involved in, make sure that you do your best.

September 11th, Monday

You may be missing out today if you don't keep your eyes open as something very good will come your way. Try not to let it pass you by. Someone may be trying to get your attention. It would be to your advantage if you show them interest even if you don't care about what they say.

September 12th, Tuesday

Today will be full of fun and adventure. This will be the start of a completely new project in which you will want to be involved. Get ready to cover new ground and learn many new things. You will have a real eye-opener today. Enjoy it while it lasts as you will not forget what you have been shown.

September 13th, Wednesday

You may be very undecided today over something that you want to buy. If you are not sure, don't take it home as it may not be as useful as you first thought. So, before you part with your money, put it through a lot of tests as you don't want to be stuck with a useless article.

September 14th, Thursday

You may feel like walking away from the situation that you are in, but try not give up as you may be in a different frame of mind tomorrow. Love matters may be getting you down and adding to your problems, but if you look at your life closely things are not as bad as they may seem. In certain ways you are lucky and you will come to realise this at the end of the day.

September 15th, Friday
You may remember a dream that you had last night, but try not to let it disturb you as nothing bad is about to happen. Sit back, put up those feet, and relax. After all, you deserve it.

September 16th, Saturday
What a day this will be. It will start off rather strangely and this sense of unreality will continue throughout the day. Let your hair down as you'll need a rather relaxed approach. Today runs very smoothly and you'll be in a good frame of mind. It will be a good day if you are dealing with people.

September 17th, Sunday
This is a new day with a new direction and you will be more than pleased with what happens today. You are certainly in for a treat. You will find that a cheerful atmosphere surrounds you and that you will receive good news. It may be something that you have been waiting for, but try not to get overexcited as you may wear yourself out.

September 18th, Monday
If you find out a home truth today, don't act on impulse as you may get the wrong impression. Find out all the facts before you take action. Someone may phone you and you may not be interested in what they have to say. Grin and bear it as they may just have some news which will cast a different light on your situation.

September 19th, Tuesday

Something that you hear on the radio will amuse you. Whatever you have on your mind to do you should carry out as you will not regret any moves that you make today. If you are thinking of making any home improvements, this would be a good time to start the ball rolling.

September 20th, Wednesday

You may feel quite alone today, but don't worry as help is at hand. Someone you didn't expect to gives you advice comes to the rescue. After you receive the advice you will know which direction to take. This will ensure that you are heading for a better future.

September 21st, Thursday

Don't be afraid to make changes as this will be a time in your life when things really start to go your way. You may have had a run of bad luck, but you must put it behind you as better luck is on its way.

September 22nd, Friday

Changes are all around you. Good luck surrounds you and nothing will be out of your reach today. If you have had any problems on the work front, this will be the perfect day to sort them out.

September 23rd, Saturday

You should be in a better frame of mind today. If you look back at the past week, you will realise that you got a lot of work done and you will have less on your mind. Love matters are set to improve and, if you are single, this will be a good time to meet that perfect love. Plan a night out on the town. It will work wonders.

September 24th, Sunday

Planetary influences indicate that new people are about to enter your life and will open many new doors for you. New friends will be made, too, and with new friends comes new money. This will make your life less complicated and this will ensure that you will have no more problems.

September 25th, Monday

Someone from your past may walk back into your life and you should not take what they tell you to heart as they may have an ulterior motive for getting in contact with you. Be sure not to commit yourself to this person as you will have no time for them in the near future. Your life will get a little hectic and you'll be in big demand.

September 26th, Tuesday

You may be faced with a very unusual situation and may not know just what to do for the best. However, at the last moment it will all work out for the best and you'll certainly be thankful to be out of the situation that you got yourself into. Now that it is all clear you can do better for yourself. You will now definitely take a huge leap forward. You will be amazed with just what is around the corner.

September 27th, Wednesday

You may feel like walking away from a current love, but would this be the right thing to do? It would not be wise to act on impulse. Take a break and have a good think before you act. Your mind will then be clear and you will know exactly what to do.

September 28th, Thursday

Someone may be pulling you back with their depressing attitude. It will do you no good to stay in such negative company as they will only bring you down. Give some other friends a call and you'll soon be feeling cheerful again.

September 29th, Friday
You will have the opportunity to rid yourself of something that you have wanted to get out of your life. Once you sort things out you will never look back and you will definitely not have any regrets. You will find that certain things that are happening are working out very well.

September 30th, Saturday
You'll probably be very pleased that this month is nearly over as it has been a bit hectic. However, better times lie directly ahead and you will be all the wiser for what you have been through. Get ready for a good month as the coming month will bring new directions and happiness into your life.

OCTOBER

October 1st, Sunday

Make your thoughts clear to a partner or family member as they may expect a little more than you can give at the moment. You may be very tired of the arguments that surround you, but the air will be cleared very soon and nobody will be left in the dark. You will then know just where everybody stands and the problem will be resolved.

October 2nd, Monday

You may feel unsettled with your work surroundings, but the situation will soon work out to your advantage. A letter that you receive today will not make your problems any worse, but will only encourage you to work harder at getting things right.

October 3rd, Tuesday

If you have a secret, now is the right time to share it. A loved one or close friend will be amused with your story and at the same time you will get things off your chest.

October 4th, Wednesday

You may think that today will be no different from the rest, but to your surprise it will turn out to be very exciting and will hold more than you ever expected. This will be the beginning of not only a new friendship but a whole new direction.

October 5th, Thursday

If the door bell rings, you'll be amazed with who is there. Planetary influences indicate that old friends or lovers will get in contact with you. You'll soon catch up with the news of their past and you may be a little surprised at just what they have been up to.

October 6th, Friday

You may feel like going on a shopping spree today and this will do you the world of good. You may feel the need to treat yourself. Why not? After all, you deserve it.

October 7th, Saturday

You may receive a letter from abroad. The good news will cheer you up and you'll be seeing someone whom you have not set eyes on for a long time.

October 8th, Sunday

Money matters that have been worrying you lately will improve and good news comes from a family member. This will improve your life and bring much happiness.

October 9th, Monday

You will hear news of money that is due to you. However, try not to spend it before you receive it as it may take a little longer to reach your bank account than you anticipated. However, the money will reach you in the end and you'll have less cause to worry.

October 10th, Tuesday

A family member will bring very good news and there may be plans to have a celebration. This may come at a very inconvenient time, but try to put a little time aside to join in with the family fun. You won't regret it.

October 11th, Wednesday

You may see something that you want to buy and now would be the right time to buy it. Listen to yourself for once and do what you really want to do. You'll certainly be pleased with what your lover or friends think. Go on, treat yourself! You only live once.

October 12th, Thursday

You may be in rather a bad mood today, but as the day progresses this mood will lift and you will then see the funny side of things. This is a good day for trying to get in touch with people who are rather elusive. This will also prove to be a day where you really get things done.

October 13th, Friday

This may be a good omen for you. Just because it's Friday the 13th does not mean that your world will come crashing down. In fact, the opposite will be true, as a new direction will open up for you. This will be that day when you see the light and change your mind about matters that have been preying on your mind.

October 14th, Saturday

You may feel a little worried over a long-standing family problem. However, all will be resolved and sooner than you think. You must try not to worry so much as this does not help your situation. You will be pleased to know you will be having better luck and money matters are set to improve.

October 15th, Sunday

You may have been searching for something special and you may feel like giving up the search. Don't give in just yet as you never know just what is around the corner. I can assure you that there are very good times to come.

October 16th, Monday

You will have a change of mind about the direction that your life is currently taking. However, try not to be too quick to change certain matters as your life is set to change for the better of its own accord.

October 17th, Tuesday

Today will prove to be quite an adventure. You will make friends with someone who is very high up in the business world. This may give your career an extra boost. You may also hear some scandal on the grapevine. You must not repeat this as it may be very misleading.

October 18th, Wednesday

Today may pass very quickly and you may wonder just where the time went. However, you may also find that you have managed to get a lot done. Planetary influences indicate that you will be the receiver of some very good news.

October 19th, Thursday

Someone near to you may think that they have everything under control. However, you may just be in the right place at the right time to step in and save the day for them. You will receive much praise and this will put you back in the spotlight.

October 20th, Friday

You can make a difference to your life if you put your mind to it, but you may need a little shove now and again. It's high time that you started to push yourself forward a little. After all, you do not really want someone else to take the credit.

October 21st, Saturday

You may have to let something go. This may feel as if you are taking a step back, but you really are taking a step forward. The loss will be a blessing in disguise and you will soon feel at home with the changes that you have just experienced.

October 22nd, Sunday

You may be surrounded by people who take pleasure in putting others down. Ignore them as they may be feeling a little jealous about someone's success. Love matters may need a little attention. It's time you cut down on a few of those luxuries.

October 23rd, Monday

Listen to your heart today. You may feel the need to move in a new direction, but you just don't know where to start. You must take one day at a time and, if it's to be, then you'll certainly go in the direction that you wish. A new chapter of your life will open.

October 24th, Tuesday

You may be feeling a little nostalgic and the past will be playing on your mind. You cannot turn back the clocks, but you can certainly make sure that you don't make the same mistake twice.

October 25th, Wednesday

Someone may be on your mind. If you are worried, pick up the phone and give them a call. You'll soon find out that everything is OK and you have been worrying for nothing. You'll be surprised just how well things are going. At least this will put your mind at rest.

October 26th, Thursday

You may be very tempted to do something out of the ordinary, but are you sure that you are not getting yourself into a situation that you will not get out of so easily? Have a good think about it and ask yourself if it is really worth it. If it is, then go ahead.

October 27th, Friday

You may be running late today with certain matters in your life. Don't worry as when you put your mind to it you will certainly catch up. You'll get more done than you think.

October 28th, Saturday

If you have encountered any problems, you will be sure to win through today. If you do not give up, you will win in the end. You are right to persevere as you will make great headway. Money matters may be on your mind, but tackle your bank balance at a later date.

October 29th, Sunday

You may feel as if there is something better in life and you may feel at a low ebb. You should take a good look around you as you are just feeling negative today. Your life will soon change on its own accord and you will be pleased with the outcome of your present situation. You will also be very pleased that you did not make any hasty decisions.

October 30th, Monday

Put your feet up today and relax. Watch TV and let your mind wander. Try not to think about your worries today. Leave them where they belong. Push them into tomorrow as tomorrow never comes.

October 31st, Tuesday

A new door will open today, but you may be nervous or just hesitant about which direction you could take. The opportunity that opens up for you will be so tempting that you will know deep down that it is the right direction to take.

NOVEMBER

November 1st, Wednesday

You may be quick to judge a stranger today, but you should give them the benefit of the doubt. You may find that you have judged them wrongly and that they will turn out to be very different from what you first thought.

November 2nd, Thursday

You will find out something that you have wanted to know for some time. Use this knowledge wisely and you will benefit from it. You can also use this to help you with your love life. If you have any plans to improve your love life, you now have the magic bullets. Use them wisely and you will not go far wrong.

November 3rd, Friday

You may meet a complete stranger and you will feel that you have known them all your life. No doubt you will stay good friends for a long time so take some time to get to know them.

November 4th, Saturday

You may be putting yourself down in many ways. Try not to put yourself down. You need to be more positive as you are about to enter a new chapter in your life. This will open your eyes to many opportunities that you may take in the near future.

November 5th, Sunday

Your life should now be moving into the fast lane and you may find that it may be going a little too fast for you. However, it will not stay in the fast lane and will slow to a more comfortable speed. You should expect to make new friends and move on to higher ground.

November 6th, Monday

You may be thinking of putting a keep-fit plan into action. This would be the perfect time to do so. Try to spend a little more time with a loved one as they may be feeling a little down.

November 7th, Tuesday

You may be thinking about cash that you have recently spent. There is no point in crying over spilt milk. Don't worry as you will manage easily as some money will come to you from an unexpected source.

November 8th, Wednesday

You may be feeling rather inquisitive, but try not to put your nose where it's not wanted. If you overhear any gossip, it would be in your own interest to keep it to yourself.

November 9th, Thursday

You may be buying unnecessary items today. Try not to waste your money as you'll need it for more important matters. You may be wasting time with a work situation. Try a different approach and this will work wonders and give a boost to your image.

November 10th, Friday

You may feel fed up with a certain family member, but if you speak your mind you could do long-term damage. Try to keep calm and all will be well. On the whole time will go fast today and too many things may happen. Try to keep control of your emotions.

November 11th, Saturday

Today will prove to be more than successful and you'll find out that you will be on the receiving end of some very good news. News about money matters will come to your attention. You will be planning to have a celebration in the near future.

November 12th, Sunday

Someone may drop a bombshell today and this may not please you. Try to look deeper into the situation as you may find that things are not really as bad as they seem. The problem that is facing you will soon fade into the past.

November 13th, Monday

A shopping spree may be on the cards today. Try not to spend too much as you may find that you will go over budget. You must cut down a little as you will need money for another time. Try to keep a little to one side as you will need a little extra cash in the future

November 14th, Tuesday

You may be having a disagreement with a loved one. Try not to say things that you don't really mean as you may regret hurting your loved one's feelings. Try to calm the situation down. You'll find that it will soon be over and happiness will return to your life.

November 15th, Wednesday

You may be told a secret from which you will benefit greatly. This will put you on guard in a future situation if someone hints about what you have been told. On no account let on that you know.

November 16th, Thursday

If you are worrying over a family matter, you will be pleased to know that this problem will soon be solved and all your worries will be over. Try not to waste your time worrying about things that may never happen.

November 17th, Friday

Today will prove to be more than just another Friday. You will make good progress and the hard work that you have put in will finally pay off. You will feel as if a black cloud that has been hanging over you has finally disappeared.

November 18th, Saturday

Your life will be moving on to bigger and better things and you will be amazed at what happens around you. Life should be more settled and you will find that you are in a good frame of mind.

November 19th, Sunday

You may have to take a step back before you can move forwards. This will ensure that you move in a better direction. You should not let changes unsettle you.

November 20th, Monday

Planetary influences indicate that you will move into a new phase of your life today and the changes that you encounter will bring contentment into your life. A loved one may express their feelings to you and tell you certain things that are on their mind. Try to sort out your differences and you'll reach a better understanding.

November 21st, Tuesday

You may have a little more free time on your hands and you may wonder just what to do with yourself. Try something that you would not usually do. You will find this very interesting and you may find that it will broaden your horizons.

November 22nd, Wednesday

The past may come flooding back to your mind and you'll be thinking of certain events that happened. Try not to recreate your past as it would not feel the same. Look to your future and you'll find better times lie ahead.

November 23rd, Thursday

A letter that you receive today will bring good news. You may have to make certain plans and change some that you have already made, but this will be for the best and you'll benefit in more ways than one.

November 24th, Friday

A decision may lie before you today and you may be hesitant about making changes. If you do not know which direction to take, think things through before you act. If you are still not sure, don't make the decision today. The right answer will come to you on another day.

November 25th, Saturday

A good change is on the cards today and you will meet someone whom you have heard all about but never actually met. This person will leave a lasting impression on you and will inspire you in a number of ways. Only good will come out of this meeting and a new door opens. Life will improve.

November 26th, Sunday

A loved one may be on the warpath. Try not to take their bait as things may blow up out of proportion. Keep your distance and the situation will soon pass and you can have a good laugh about it. However, all will be well in the end.

November 27th, Monday

A work situation may be on your mind. You will make good progress and catch up on any lost time. Try not to be side-tracked today as you may be tempted to do other things. Keep your mind on what you have to do and you'll benefit greatly.

November 28th, Tuesday

You will find yourself wanting to go out and about today as you may be feeling a little restless. Don't; you will only have the urge to spend money. You will find the odd bargain so it may be worth your while to go shopping. You will have a rather pleasant evening to look forward to, so make the best of the evening and this will add sparkle to your life.

November 29th, Wednesday

Listen to your inner feelings today. You may be hesitant in starting a project that you need to get off the ground. If you are not sure just exactly what to do, ask a close friend. They'll certainly be able to give you good advice.

November 30th, Thursday

If you feel as if there is something missing from your life, you could come across it today. Today will be very lucky for you and after the day is over you will move on to bigger and better things.

DECEMBER

December 1st, Friday

A loved one may have plans, but they may not be to your liking. Speak your mind now as it will save you any aggravation in the near future.

December 2nd, Saturday

If you had a vivid dream last night, this will be a good omen for you. Positive changes are about to take place and money matters that have been on your mind will be resolved.

December 3rd, Sunday

You may receive a phone call from a friend. You will be overjoyed with what you are told and advancement beyond your wildest dreams will come about. You may feel like celebrating, but keep this news under your hat for a while.

December 4th, Monday

A family member may need your advice. Try to make time for them as they may be at a low point in their life. This may cause you some worry, but all will come out in the wash and will be easily sorted out.

December 5th, Tuesday

You may find yourself in strange surroundings today. This will lead to an adventure. Planetary influences indicate that you will be mixing in a different social circle and this will take your life in another direction for a while. However, nothing but good will come out of this.

December 6th, Wednesday

You may have Christmas on your mind. This may be a good time to make a list and make a start with thinking about presents. This will save you time and money as, if you start early, you will have no cause to panic later.

December 7th, Thursday

Someone from your past may try to get in contact with you. It would be in your best interest not to arrange to meet up as there is more to it than meets the eye. Decline their offer and very soon you'll find out their real motive. You will be glad that you were cautious.

December 8th, Friday

Money matters will improve today and this may be a good time to open a new bank account or think about a pension plan. Any money invested now will double in time and pay large dividends.

December 9th, Saturday

You may feel as if your life is on hold today in certain aspects. You may get extra inspiration from your immediate surroundings. If you have planned travel or a business move, now is the time to act as planetary influences indicate that luck will be on your side.

December 10th, Sunday

People close to you may be telling you their worries and troubles. Don't take them to heart as they are probably just having a good grumble as you are an easy person to talk to. There is news of a birth in the near future and a family member may be planning a move.

December 11th, Monday

Your life will return to normality today. Planetary influences have hindered you and pulled you back a little. Exciting matters are about to come to a head. Your life is about to move into the fast lane. Get ready for the ride of a lifetime. You will not forget it in a hurry.

December 12th, Tuesday

Someone who wears black will bring you good luck and a big change is foreseen. A stranger brings money closer to your bank account. A phone call that you receive today will please you greatly. Family problems that you have encountered will be resolved and new foundations will be laid.

December 13th, Wednesday

Take time out to have a little fun. Try going somewhere that you have never been before. You may have had your eye on that certain something for some time now. This is the right time to treat yourself. Money matters will improve and a better position within a work situation is foreseen.

December 14th, Thursday

Something that you have wanted in the past will now be within your reach. Don't be influenced by others. Follow your heart and you will have no problems. You may have to throw yourself in at the deep end with a business matter before you make any headway. This will be a day when you really get things done and you will get a project off the ground.

December 15th, Friday

You may ask yourself where you go from here. However, just as you give up hope, a new direction will appear right before your eyes. You must not give in to a negative frame of mind as this will do you no good.

December 16th, Saturday

You may have the urge to take up some sort of sport. A new idea may suddenly come to you. Put it down on paper as it will bring many good things and open many new doors for you in the near future.

December 17th, Sunday

A wish that you have made in the past will finally come true today. Try to have a little more understanding with a family member as you may have been a little too strict with them in the past. Hear them out and then take the appropriate action.

December 18th, Monday

This will prove to be a very propitious day and you will be over the moon with a partner as there will be very good news on the way. Something that you hear on the radio will interest you and put you in a very good mood.

December 19th, Tuesday

You may need to pay a little attention to a family matter, but this is not necessarily bad. This will bring many good times into your family life. Plans made today will definitely come to fruition.

December 20th, Wednesday

You will overcome any obstacles that stand in your way today. This is the perfect day to get ahead with any household problems. Love is starred well and it looks as if you are in for a bit of a treat tonight.

December 21st, Thursday

This will be the day that your luck changes for the better and things start to finally go your way. Certain things that you have tried to do have not been so easy in the past. This will definitely make a change. More changes at work are indicated.

December 22nd, Friday

A travel plan may have to be changed at the last minute, but this will turn out for the best. A work colleague may help you in more ways than one. You may find it a little odd that they are going out of their way to help you. There may be a method in their madness, but just play along with them as you will only benefit from their helping hand.

December 23rd, Saturday
You will be in the right time at the right place today and you will be pleased with the result of what today brings. You must be positive and not be afraid to air your views. You certainly will not regret any decisions that you make today.

December 24th, Sunday
You may find yourself doing a last-minute dash for those last bits and pieces. Try not to panic as you will not forget something important. Take your time; you will get more done. This evening will bring a real surprise and you will not regret what takes place. You will not forget today in a hurry.

December 25th, Monday
Happy Christmas! You will be more than pleased with what you receive, but most of all you will be pleased with the outcome of today. People whom you care about most will surround you and good times lie ahead.

December 26th, Tuesday
If you are feeling a little down, try not to worry as you'll soon be feeling better. A good day is foreseen. Love matters will finally be resolved and better times lie ahead for the romantic side of your life. Try to have a little rest as you are set for an exciting evening. You'll be in the spotlight today.

December 27th, Wednesday
Do your own thing today and you will not go far wrong. People may tend to annoy you today, but try not to play into their hands. A good atmosphere will surround you this evening and a real surprise is in store.

December 28th, Thursday

Don't think about past events as this will not do you any good. Put the past to the back of your mind as such thoughts will only spoil your day. You will be making plans for the future and what is planned today will come to pass for sure.

December 29th, Friday

You will be entering a new chapter of your life and what takes place today will certainly open your eyes. Look around you and you may realise just what you have taken for granted. A good day will be had and you will make good progress.

December 30th, Saturday

If you have a few tasks to get out of the way, try not to rush around as this will not make your life any easier. Take time out to do the things that you enjoy most. You will find yourself having a lot of fun. You may find yourself thinking of the past, but you have a brighter future to look forward to and better luck is about to come your way.

December 31st, Sunday

This is the last day of the year and you will be celebrating in style. When the bells ring at midnight you may feel relieved that this year has finally come to its close.

As for the coming year, you have some very good opportunities on the horizon and planetary influences indicate that major changes are ahead. On the whole you can look forward to a good year ahead of you.

♏

IMPORTANT DATES
2000

IMPORTANT DATES
2000

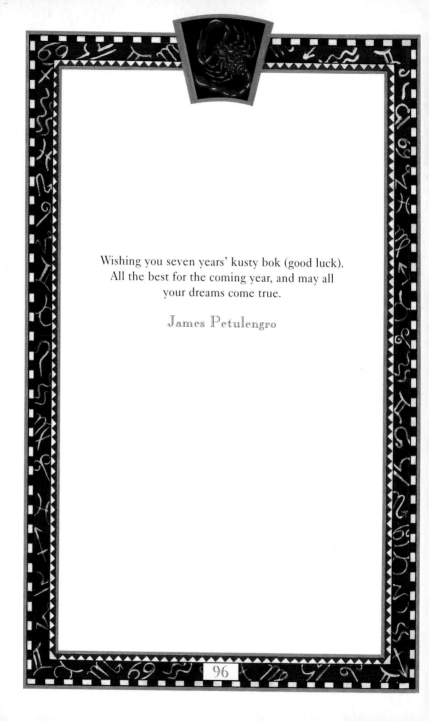

Wishing you seven years' kusty bok (good luck).
All the best for the coming year, and may all
your dreams come true.

James Petulengro